The Sun looks good on you

31 Day Inspiration Journal

Dear Reader,

I wrote this short inspiration journal as I began my own personal creative journey. I knew that in order for me to begin the journey and stay committed I needed to be inspired.

I have included quotes, questions, and personal anecdotes to help you on your journey.

My hope is that as I reveal what I have learned, it will spark creativity and unravel truth in your own life.

DAY 1

Write down your vision.

There is something powerful about writing down what it is you want to accomplish. It activates faith and is a catalyst for making your visions come alive.

What is your vision for your life? Where do you see yourself?

_____

_____

_____

_____

_____

_____

_____

_____

_____

_____

_____

_____

The Sun looks good on you

DAY 2

Fear has stolen faith from every generation. It is the greatest thief lurking in our spines.

What are you afraid of?
How many of your decisions are made out of fear?

_____

_____

_____

_____

_____

_____

_____

_____

_____

_____

_____

_____

_____

The Sun looks good on you

_____

_____

_____

_____

_____

_____

_____

_____

_____

_____

_____

_____

_____

_____

_____

_____

_____

_____

DAY 3

Faith is a key that unlocks doors few dare to open.

What doors do you hope will open once you step
out in faith?

_____

_____

_____

_____

_____

_____

_____

_____

_____

_____

_____

The Sun looks good on you

_____

_____

_____

_____

_____

_____

_____

_____

_____

_____

_____

_____

_____

_____

DAY 4

God did not call you to conform.

There is this subtle and at times obvious tug on us all to look the same, dress the same, and think the same. The truth is that you are different for a reason.

In what ways were you taught to conform? How has that shaped you?

_____

_____

_____

_____

_____

_____

_____

_____

_____

_____

_____

_____

_____

_____

_____

_____

_____

_____

_____

_____

_____

_____

_____

_____

_____

_____

DAY 5

We exemplify God in our uniqueness.

You offer to the world what no one else can: yourself.

In what ways are you different? How do you feel about your uniqueness?

_____

_____

_____

_____

_____

_____

_____

_____

_____

_____

_____

The Sun looks good on you

_____

_____

_____

_____

_____

_____

_____

_____

_____

_____

_____

_____

_____

_____

_____

_____

Day 6

Your voice matters. Your truth matters.

What have you always wanted to say but never said?

_____

_____

_____

_____

_____

_____

_____

_____

_____

_____

_____

_____

The Sun looks good on you

_____

_____

_____

_____

_____

_____

_____

_____

_____

_____

_____

_____

_____

_____

_____

Day 7

Pursue your passions.

What are you most passionate about? What brings you joy?

_____

_____

_____

_____

_____

_____

_____

_____

_____

_____

_____

_____

_____

The Sun looks good on you

_____

_____

_____

_____

_____

_____

_____

_____

_____

_____

_____

_____

_____

_____

_____

Day 8

You don't have to be amazing or perfect just a vessel to be used.

In your imperfections, how are you being used for a greater purpose?

_____

_____

_____

_____

_____

_____

_____

_____

_____

_____

_____

_____

The Sun looks good on you

_____

_____

_____

_____

_____

_____

_____

_____

_____

_____

_____

_____

_____

_____

_____

Day 9

Don't be afraid of failure.

Failures are lessons life teaches us so that we may grow and be successful.

In what ways are you afraid to fail? What has failure taught you in the past?

_____

_____

_____

_____

_____

_____

_____

_____

_____

_____

_____

The Sun looks good on you

_____

_____

_____

_____

_____

_____

_____

_____

_____

_____

_____

_____

_____

_____

Day 10

The day I stopped worrying about people's opinions of me was the day I began living.

Whose opinions matter to you? Why?

_____

_____

_____

_____

_____

_____

_____

_____

_____

_____

_____

The Sun looks good on you

_____

_____

_____

_____

_____

_____

_____

_____

_____

_____

_____

_____

_____

_____

Day 11

Invest in yourself.

You are a great investment. Remind yourself daily.

How are you investing in yourself? What does investing in yourself look like for you?

_____

_____

_____

_____

_____

_____

_____

_____

_____

_____

_____

_____

The Sun looks good on you

Day 12

Be patient with yourself. You are still learning.

What are your challenges? How are you extending
grace to yourself daily?

_____

_____

_____

_____

_____

_____

_____

_____

_____

_____

The Sun looks good on you

_____

_____

_____

_____

_____

_____

_____

_____

_____

_____

_____

_____

_____

_____

_____

_____

Day 13

Rejoice in others' accomplishments.

Having the mindset: 'I am blessed when they are blessed' frees you to experience greater joy in your own life.

Who has experienced a great accomplishment/milestone in your circle? Are you truly happy for them?

_____

_____

_____

_____

_____

_____

_____

_____

_____

_____

The Sun looks good on you

Day 14

Envy is the greatest enemy to true community.

How has envy impacted your friendships in the
past or currently affects your relationships?

_____

_____

_____

_____

_____

_____

_____

_____

_____

_____

_____

The Sun looks good on you

_____

_____

_____

_____

_____

_____

_____

_____

_____

_____

_____

_____

_____

_____

_____

_____

Day 15

Revelation is revealed in rest.

Take a day to rest and relax. What was revealed to
you in your time of rest?

_____

_____

_____

_____

_____

_____

_____

_____

_____

_____

_____

The Sun looks good on you

_____

_____

_____

_____

_____

_____

_____

_____

_____

_____

_____

_____

_____

_____

_____

Day 16

Breathe.

Take a deep breath in. And a deep breath out.
Repeat.

_____

_____

_____

_____

_____

_____

_____

_____

_____

_____

_____

_____

_____

The Sun looks good on you

_____

_____

_____

_____

_____

_____

_____

_____

_____

_____

_____

_____

_____

_____

_____

_____

Day 17

Renewed minds lead to transformed lives.

What mindsets do you need to let go? How can this change your life?

_____

_____

_____

_____

_____

_____

_____

_____

_____

_____

_____

The Sun looks good on you

_____

_____

_____

_____

_____

_____

_____

_____

_____

_____

_____

_____

_____

_____

_____

_____

Day 18

Time is the only commodity that cannot be added, only spent.

How are you spending your time? What areas should you invest more time in or less time?

_____

_____

_____

_____

_____

_____

_____

_____

_____

_____

_____

_____

The Sun looks good on you

_____

_____

_____

_____

_____

_____

_____

_____

_____

_____

_____

_____

_____

_____

_____

_____

_____

Day 19

Stay committed to the journey.

I have discovered that the process is a part of the plan and the journey is really the destination.

What has your journey looked like so far?

_____

_____

_____

_____

_____

_____

_____

_____

_____

_____

_____

The Sun looks good on you

_____

_____

_____

_____

_____

_____

_____

_____

_____

_____

_____

_____

_____

_____

_____

Day 20

Consistency is key.

Success is often not given to the most talented, but to the ones that never gave up.

How have you been consistent in pursuing your dreams? What is your biggest hindrance in staying consistent?

_____

_____

_____

_____

_____

_____

_____

_____

_____

_____

_____

The Sun looks good on you

_____

_____

_____

_____

_____

_____

_____

_____

_____

_____

_____

_____

_____

_____

Day 21

Stop hiding in the shadows.
Come into the light and shine.
Like all stars do.

What talents do you possess? In what areas do you shine?

_____

_____

_____

_____

_____

_____

_____

_____

_____

_____

_____

_____

The Sun looks good on you

_____

_____

_____

_____

_____

_____

_____

_____

_____

_____

_____

_____

_____

_____

_____

_____

Day 22

Use your platform whether big or small.

We can all get caught up in the numbers game on social media: counting the number of 'friends' 'followers', 'likes' and 'comments'. We forget the power of sharing your gifts with even one person.

What is your platform? How can you use your gifts on your current platform?

The Sun looks good on you

_____

_____

_____

_____

_____

_____

_____

_____

_____

_____

_____

_____

_____

_____

_____

_____

Day 23

Believe in yourself even when it feels like no one else does.

Do you believe in yourself? What do you hope to accomplish?

_____

_____

_____

_____

_____

_____

_____

_____

_____

_____

_____

_____

The Sun looks good on you

_____

_____

_____

_____

_____

_____

_____

_____

_____

_____

_____

_____

_____

_____

_____

_____

_____

Day 24

Experience and Exposure are invaluable.

Sometimes you won't get paid much for your work. Humble yourself and accept these invitations as opportunities for experience and growth.

What experiences have you gained in the past?
How has it sharpened your craft?

_____

_____

_____

_____

_____

_____

_____

_____

_____

_____

_____

1

The Sun looks good on you

_____

_____

_____

_____

_____

_____

_____

_____

_____

_____

_____

_____

_____

_____

_____

_____

Day 25

Even the God of the universe exists in community.

We need each other to do the things we are
purposed to do and become the people we need to be.

How has community helped you in your creative
journey?

_____

_____

_____

_____

_____

_____

_____

_____

_____

_____

_____

The Sun looks good on you

_____

_____

_____

_____

_____

_____

_____

_____

_____

_____

_____

_____

_____

_____

_____

_____

Day 26

Surround yourself with people that remind you how blessed you are.

Who are your friends? What do they mean to you?

_____

_____

_____

_____

_____

_____

_____

_____

_____

_____

_____

_____

The Sun looks good on you

_____

_____

_____

_____

_____

_____

_____

_____

_____

_____

_____

_____

_____

_____

_____

Day 27

Dreams never age.

What are your dreams? What do you wish to
accomplish? Create?

_____

_____

_____

_____

_____

_____

_____

_____

_____

_____

_____

_____

The Sun looks good on you

_____

_____

_____

_____

_____

_____

_____

_____

_____

_____

_____

_____

_____

_____

_____

Day 28

People may perish but legacies never die.

What legacy do you hope to leave behind? How are you working toward creating that legacy?

_____

_____

_____

_____

_____

_____

_____

_____

_____

_____

_____

_____

The Sun looks good on you

_____

_____

_____

_____

_____

_____

_____

_____

_____

_____

_____

_____

_____

_____

_____

Day 29

God cares about your growth more than your comfort.

In what areas do you feel you need to grow? How often do you get out of your comfort zone?

_____

_____

_____

_____

_____

_____

_____

_____

_____

_____

_____

_____

The Sun looks good on you

_____

_____

_____

_____

_____

_____

_____

_____

_____

_____

_____

_____

_____

_____

Day 30

Your purpose is a person: you.

Your purpose is you becoming the person you were created to be.

How are you pursuing yourself and your gifts?

_____

_____

_____

_____

_____

_____

_____

_____

_____

_____

_____

_____

The Sun looks good on you

_____

_____

_____

_____

_____

_____

_____

_____

_____

_____

_____

_____

_____

_____

_____

_____

Day 31

Pursuing purpose is when your greatest passion meets a great need.

What are you most passionate about? How does this serve the world?

_____

_____

_____

_____

_____

_____

_____

_____

_____

_____

_____

The Sun looks good on you

_____

_____

_____

_____

_____

_____

_____

_____

_____

_____

_____

_____

_____

_____

_____

_____

_____

_____

_____

_____

_____

_____

_____

_____

_____

_____

_____

_____

_____

_____

_____

_____

_____

The Sun looks good on you

_____

_____

_____

_____

_____

_____

_____

_____

_____

_____

_____

_____

_____

_____

_____

_____

The Sun looks good on you

_____

_____

_____

_____

_____

_____

_____

_____

_____

_____

_____

_____

_____

_____

The Sun looks good on you

_____

_____

_____

_____

_____

_____

_____

_____

_____

_____

_____

_____

_____

_____

_____

_____

The Sun looks good on you

The Sun looks good on you

_____

_____

_____

_____

_____

_____

_____

_____

_____

_____

_____

_____

_____

_____

_____

_____

The Sun looks good on you

_____

_____

_____

_____

_____

_____

_____

_____

_____

_____

_____

_____

_____

_____

_____

_____

The Sun looks good on you

_____

_____

_____

_____

_____

_____

_____

_____

_____

_____

_____

_____

_____

The Sun looks good on you

_____

_____

_____

_____

_____

_____

_____

_____

_____

_____

_____

_____

_____

_____

The Sun looks good on you

_____

_____

_____

_____

_____

_____

_____

_____

_____

_____

_____

_____

_____

_____

_____

_____

The Sun looks good on you

The Sun looks good on you

_____

_____

_____

_____

_____

_____

_____

_____

_____

_____

_____

_____

_____

_____

_____

The Sun looks good on you

_____

_____

_____

_____

_____

_____

_____

_____

_____

_____

_____

_____

_____

_____

_____

_____

The Sun looks good on you

_____

_____

_____

_____

_____

_____

_____

_____

_____

_____

_____

_____

_____

_____

The Sun looks good on you

The Sun looks good on you

_____

_____

_____

_____

_____

_____

_____

_____

_____

_____

_____

_____

_____

_____

_____

_____

The Sun looks good on you

_____

_____

_____

_____

_____

_____

_____

_____

_____

_____

_____

_____

_____

_____

The Sun looks good on you

_____

_____

_____

_____

_____

_____

_____

_____

_____

_____

_____

_____

_____

_____

The Sun looks good on you

_____

_____

_____

_____

_____

_____

_____

_____

_____

_____

_____

_____

_____

_____

_____

The Sun looks good on you

_____

_____

_____

_____

_____

_____

_____

_____

_____

_____

_____

_____

_____

_____

_____

The Sun looks good on you

The Sun looks good on you

The Sun looks good on you

The Sun looks good on you

_____

_____

_____

_____

_____

_____

_____

_____

_____

_____

_____

_____

_____

_____

_____

The Sun looks good on you

_____

_____

_____

_____

_____

_____

_____

_____

_____

_____

_____

_____

_____

_____

ABOUT THE AUTHOR

Millicent Campbell is a Speech-Language Pathologist, poet, spoken word artist, and writer living in Houston, TX. Her greatest desire is to write with honesty, transparency, and compassion. Millicent believes that as she reveals truth in her life, audiences can write and unravel truth in their own lives.

For booking inquiries please contact
millispeakstruth@gmail.com

Made in the USA
Monee, IL
19 July 2020

36740720R00059